The Sixth
Anti-Coloring
Book®

Susan Striker

An Owl Book

Henry Holt and Company   New York

Owl Books
Henry Holt and Company, LLC
Publishers since 1866
175 Fifth Avenue
New York, New York 10010
www.henryholt.com

An Owl Book ® and ® are registered
trademarks of Henry Holt and Company, LLC.

ISBN-13: 978-0-8050-7649-3
ISBN-10: 0-8050-7649-2

Henry Holt books are available for special promotions and
premiums. For details contact: Director, Special Markets.

Printed in the United States of America

10   9   8   7   6   5   4   3

Grateful acknowledgment is made to the following for
permission to reprint illustrations and lyrics: Upper-left
illustration on p. vi, from *The Ginghams on the Farm Coloring
Book*, © 1979 Western Publishing Company, Inc., reprinted
by permission. Lower-left illustration on p. vi, from *Coloring
and Fun Pad*, copyright © Sharon Publications, reprinted by
permission. Lyrics to "Flowers Are Red" by Harry Chapin,
© 1978 Chapin Music, used by permission.

The Anti-Coloring Book is a registered trademark of
Susan Striker.

Introduction

Would the forest be as beautiful if all the trees looked exactly alike? Surely the variety of shapes, sizes, textures, and colors enhances the effect. When we plant a tree, we give it water and loving care, and then we trust in nature, certain that the tree will grow in the right direction. Yet, with our children, we push and pull as they grow. We show them the "right" way to do just about everything, too seldom trusting in their abilities to discover their own right way, instead of nurturing them to grow and develop into beautiful human beings, all special and different from each other.

Art is one area of a child's life in which the error of our ways is easily seen. By about the age of seven, children begin doing subject-motivated art. If they have been given a solid groundwork in self-taught art and a familiarity with various art materials, they will embark on this new stage of development with the self-confidence necessary for effectively using art as a means of personal self-expression. On the other hand, if children's experience of art during the first seven years has been directed by adults —or, worse still, if it has required only robotlike back-and-forth hand movements to color in adult-made art—children will become totally dependent on adult directions and patterns.

Children quickly perceive adults' lack of interest in their early art and recognize a preference for adult art. They become so accustomed to doing art as trite holiday decoration and producing pictures pleasing to adults that by the time they are old enough to do their own subject-motivated art, they no longer have any interest in doing so. As they look to adults to be told what to make and how to make it, an important method of learning how to think independently and solve problems is lost forever. Another generation of human beings grows to adulthood completely illiterate in one of life's most important areas.

The Anti–Coloring Book series is devoted to combatting this smothering adult attitude and to helping children find their own personal reasons for creating. The drawings provide opportunities for choosing ideas that may be appealing, while setting others aside for a different mood at another time. Thus children can learn how to overcome the dependency fostered during all of those formative years spent coloring in the lines of someone else's drawings.

It is easy to see why children quickly learn to undervalue their own art; after all, it is so very different from adult art. It may be different, but it certainly isn't inferior! The mediocre, stereotypical drawings we ask our children to sacrifice their own artwork for can't compare to the expressive drawings done by a free child. Consider the following examples. In the first set are two bedtime scenes for children to complete, one from a typical coloring book and the other from an Anti-Coloring Book. Clearly, allowing a child to express a bad dream can evoke an original image, impossible for a child who is given a saccharin, adult-drawn bedroom scene to color in neatly.

Ready for Bed

Draw the worst nightmare you ever had.

Even when the coloring-book drawing is decorative and fanciful, as it is below, it cannot compete with a child's imaginative work.

Name of fish: Capiamandis Fish
Discovered by: JAMES Lowe
Place discovered: In The Lock Ness

Scientists have just found a new species of fish, but they haven't named it yet. What do you think it looks like and what would you call it?

We do a disservice to children by feeling compelled to "teach" them things, when the lessons so often prevent them from seeing the world with their own fresh vision.

One of the late Harry Chapin's songs poignantly expresses the philosophy of the Anti–Coloring Books:

Flowers Are Red

The little boy went first day of school
He got some crayons and started to draw
He put colors all over the paper
For colors was what he saw
And the teacher said…What you doin' young man
I'm paintin' flowers he said
She said…it's not the time for art young man
And anyway flowers are green and red
There's a time for everything young man
And a way it should be done
You've got to show concern for everyone else
For you're not the only one

And she said…
Flowers are red young man
Green leaves are green
There's no need to see flowers any other way
Than the way they always have been seen
But the little boy said…
There are so many colors in the rainbow
So many colors in the mornin' sun
So many colors in a flower and I see every one
Well the teacher said…You're sassy
There's ways that things should be
And you'll paint flowers the way they are
So repeat after me…

And she said…
Flowers are red young man
Green leaves are green
There's no need to see flowers any other way
Than the way they always have been seen
But the little boy said…

There are so many colors in the rainbow
So many colors in the morning sun
So many colors in a flower
And I see every one

The teacher put him in a corner
She said…It's for your own good
And you won't come out 'til you get it right
And all responding like you should
Well finally he got lonely
Frightened thoughts filled his head
And he went up to the teacher
And this is what he said…and he said
Flowers are red, green leaves are green
There's no need to see flowers any other way
Than the way they always have been seen
Time went by like it always does
And they moved to another town
And the little boy went to another school
And this is what he found
The teacher there was smilin'
She said…Painting should be fun
And there are so many colors in a flower
So let's use every one
But that little boy painted flowers
In neat rows of green and red
And when the teacher asked him why
This is what he said…and he said
Flowers are red, green leaves are green
There's no need to see flowers any other way
Than the way they always have been seen

When you wake up in the morning, what do you most look forward to doing?

The Sixth Anti-Coloring Book® / Owl Books

Your spaceship is landing on Mars,
and the Welcoming Committee
is coming to greet you.

© Susan Striker

JASON'S TOY SHOP

If your parents said you could buy any toy you wanted, what would you choose?

Design the perfect jungle gym.

What do you think the dentist sees when you "open wide"?

You are about to film the most exciting scene in your new adventure movie.

1179J 3

What popped out of the box?

© Susan Striker

PLEASE do not feed the parents

PARENTS' HABITAT

© Susan Striker

IF YOUR MOTHER AND FATHER TURNED INTO DIFFERENT ANIMALS, WHAT DO YOU THINK THEY WOULD BE?

© Susan Striker

*Someone spilled paint
all over the ground. Can you
turn it into a picture of anything?*

Pet Shop

The Sixth Anti-Coloring Book® / Owl Books

If you could have any kind of dog,
what would you choose?

Where would you go if you were invisible?

© Susan Striker

Do a picture that you can cut up to make a jigsaw puzzle.

What would you
expect to find
while exploring
on another
planet?

The Sixth Anti-Coloring Book® / Owl Books

What if ... _____

_____

_____

_____

_____

What have you spotted up in the sky?

The Sixth Anti-Coloring Book® / Owl Books

If you had a star on your dressing-room door, what would it be for?

What is the worst thing about being a kid?

© Susan Striker

What kind of airplane would you like to build?

© Susan Striker

Where do you think balloons go when they fly away?

What would you love to get tickets for?

What do these construction
materials make you dream of building?

© Susan Striker

What was the funniest thing that ever happened to you?

What was the saddest thing that ever happened to you?

The Sixth Anti-Coloring Book® / Owl Books

NASA has asked you to design a new space shuttle.

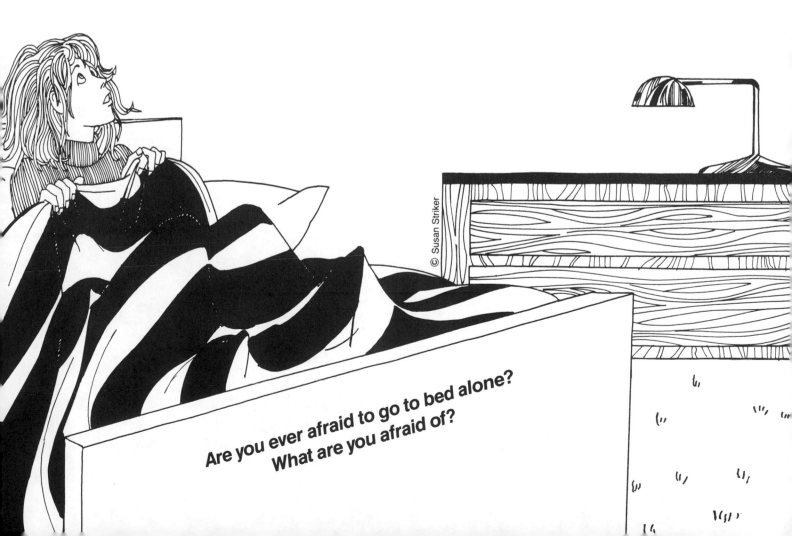

© Susan Striker

Are you ever afraid to go to bed alone?
What are you afraid of?

The Sixth Anti-Coloring Book® / Owl Books

What do you think the ground looks like from an airplane?

5¢

What surprise can you find in this bubble gum machine?

The best painting I ever did looked like this!

The Sixth Anti-Coloring Book® / Owl Books

© Susan Striker

If you were the driver, where would this car be going?

If you had your very own secret garden, how would it look?

© Susan Striker

What do you imagine your parents do all day
while you are at school?

© Susan Striker

If you broke a mirror, what would happen to you?

© Susan Striker

Design a cereal box that will be interesting to read
and look at while you eat breakfast.

These sightseers were surprised by a monster that rises from the sea every hundred years.

© Susan Striker

Make a wish as you blow the dandelion seeds away.

The Sixth Anti-Coloring Book® / Owl Books

Bravo! This is the performance that has earned a standing ovation.

What would you like to buy for your parents?

The Sixth Anti-Coloring Book® / Owl Books

© Susan Striker

If you were a machine, what would you do?

Design an exciting new arcade
video game.

©Susan Striker

What is the best thing about your birthday?

What makes you cry?

© Susan Striker

*If you were a tree, what would
you look like?*

The Sixth Anti-Coloring Book® / Owl Books

Design your own tombstone

The Sixth Anti-Coloring Book® / Owl Books

*It's summer vacation! What are you going to do
with your free time?*

The Anti-Coloring Book® by Susan Striker and Edward Kimmel
General interest, for ages 6 and older.
ISBN 0-8050-6842-2

The Second Anti-Coloring Book® by Susan Striker with Edward Kimmel
General interest, for ages 6 and older.
ISBN 0-8050-6843-0

The Third Anti-Coloring Book® by Susan Striker
General interest, for ages 6 and older.
ISBN 0-8050-7422-8

The Fourth Anti-Coloring Book® by Susan Striker
General interest, for ages 6 and older.
ISBN 0-8050-7423-6

The Fifth Anti-Coloring Book® by Susan Striker
General interest, for ages 6 and older.
ISBN 0-8050-7648-4

The Sixth Anti-Coloring Book® by Susan Striker
General interest, for ages 6 and older.
ISBN 0-8050-7649-2

The Anti-Coloring Book® *of Exploring Space on Earth* by Susan Striker
Architecture and interior design.
ISBN 0-8050-1446-2

The Anti-Coloring Book® *of Masterpieces* by Susan Striker
The world's great art, including color reproductions.
ISBN 0-8050-2644-4

The Inventor's Anti-Coloring Book® by Susan Striker
Inventions, devices, and contraptions.
ISBN 0-8050-2615-0

The Mystery Anti-Coloring Book® by Susan Striker
Mysteries, discoveries, and cops and robbers.
ISBN 0-8050-1600-7

The Newspaper Anti-Coloring Book® by Susan Striker
Write and illustrate your own newspaper.
ISBN 0-8050-1599-X

The Circus Anti-Coloring Book® by Susan Striker with Jason Striker
Clowns, acrobats, and everything else under the big top.
ISBN 0-8050-3412-9

The Anti-Coloring Book® *of Celebrations* by Susan Striker
Literature-based activities for holidays from around the world.
ISBN 0-8050-3414-5

Artists at Work by Susan Striker
A literature-based Anti-Coloring Book® on careers in art.
ISBN 0-8050-3413-7

Nature's Wonders for the Young at Art by Susan Striker
Creative activities using The Please Touch™ philosophy.
ISBN 0-8050-4806-5

Young at Art® by Susan Striker
Teaching toddlers self-expression, problem solving skills, and an appreciation for art.
ISBN 0-8050-6697-7

Look for these at your local bookstore.